Published by Gluten-Free by Jan LLC

Gluten-Free by Jan LLC
16067 NW Rondos Dr.
Portland, OR USA 97229-9239

ISBN: 979-8-9945334-2-0

Adventures at Manila Zoo

Animal Names in Tagalog

Jeanette Withington and Edith Withington

Manila Zoo

One sunny day, hip-hip-hooray!
Three best friends were on their way.
Past the gates so big and green,
To Manila Zoo, a fun-filled scene!

"ROAR!" said Ben with happy cheer.
"SPLASH!" said Edi, loud and clear.
"I want to PLAY the whole day through!"
Said Luna, off they went, yahoo!

lion - leon
leh-on

ROAR, ROAR, ROAR!

They tiptoed slow, then stopped to stare.
A golden lion lay right there.
He stretched his paws and shook his mane,
Then let out a roar like thunder and rain!
ROOOAAAR!
The kids said, "Wow!"
"He's loud but calm and sleepy now."
They whispered low and walked away,
Pretending to roar but in a quiet way.

elephant - elepante
eh-leh-pan-te

STOMP AND SPLASH!

The ground went STOMP! STOMP! left and right,
Big gray elephants came into sight!
One raised her trunk up to the sky,
SPLASH! went the water flying by!
Edi laughed, "I'm wet, oh my!"
Ben danced as drops went splish-splash-sky!
Flap-flap ears and happy feet,
Elephant play was such a treat!

duck - pato
pah-to

SPLISH, SPLASH, POND FUN

By the pond went quack, quack, quack,
Little ducks swam front and back.
Fish went swish beneath the blue,
Turtles waved a slow "hello" too.
Edi smiled and clapped with glee,
"Water friends just like the sea!"

turtle - pagong
pa-gong

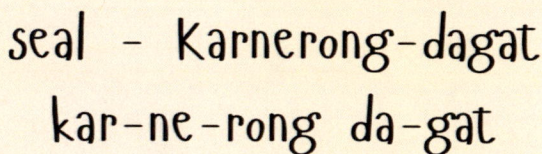

seal - Karnerong-dagat
kar-ne-rong da-gat

monkey - unggoy

ung-goy

CHATTER, CHATTER, JUMP!

Up above what do they hear?
"Eek! Eek!" monkeys swinging near!
Jumping, flipping, climbing high,
Tickling clouds up in the sky.
"Let's swing too!" the children cried,
They swung their arms and
fell-ker-plop! inside giggles wide.

giraffe - dyirap

jee-rap

SOFT STEPS, SHH...

In a shady, quiet place,
Gentle giraffe walked with soft grace.
"Munch, munch," went the leafy snack,
Brown eyes watched but didn't track.
Luna whispered, "Kind and sweet,
Soft like clouds and quiet feet."

bird – ibon
ee-bon

TIME TO PLAY

Under trees with fruit so sweet,
The friends sat down to rest their feet.
"I'm a lion, ROAR!" said Ben.
"I splash like elephants!" said Edi then.
"I swing like monkeys!" Luna cried,
They laughed and played side by side.
Birds sang songs above their heads,
Happy thoughts and sleepy threads.

GOODBYE, ZOO

The sun said bye with orange light,
The zoo grew calm and soft and bright.
"Roar, Splash, and Play," they said once more,
"What a day we all adore!"
Manila Zoo waved with stomp and cheer,
"Come back soon, my friends so dear!"
Hand in hand, they walked away,
Dreaming of another zoo-filled day.

rhinoceros - rinosero
ree-no-seh-ro

PRONUNCIATION GUIDE

lion – – – – – – – – – – – leon (lee-on)

elephant – – – – – elepante (eh-leh-pan-te)

tiger – – – – – – – – – – tigre (tee-greh)

giraffe – – – – – – – – – dyirap (jee-rap)

monkey – – – – – – – – – unggoy (ung-goy)

turtle – – – – – – – – – – pagong (pa-gong)

bird – – – – – – – – – – – ibon (ee-bon)

duck – – – – – – – – – – – pato (pha-to)

rhinoceros – – – – – rinosero (ree-no-seh-ro)

seal – – karnerong-dagat (kar-ne-rong da-gat)

Explore more books by
Jeanette Withington and Edith Withington

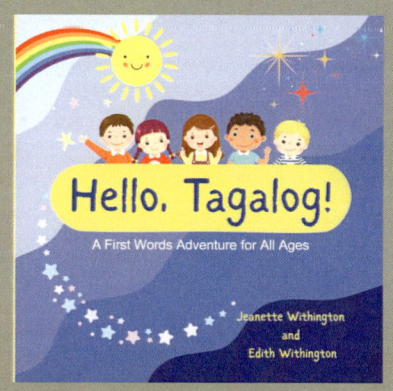

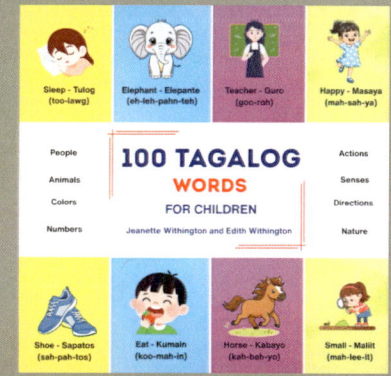

THE
END

www.ingramcontent.com/pod-product-compliance
Lightning Source LLC
Chambersburg PA
CBRC090842120626
46551CB00008B/733